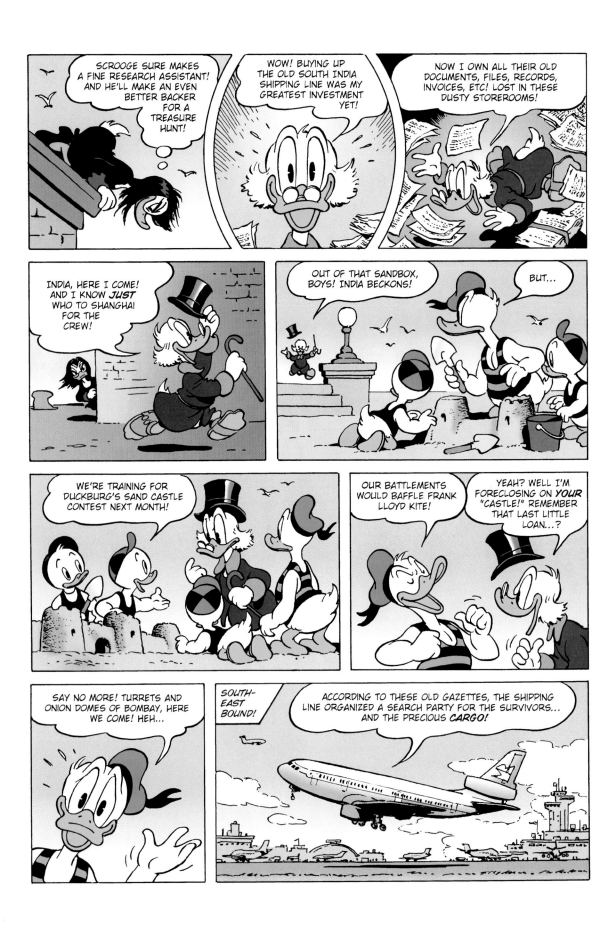

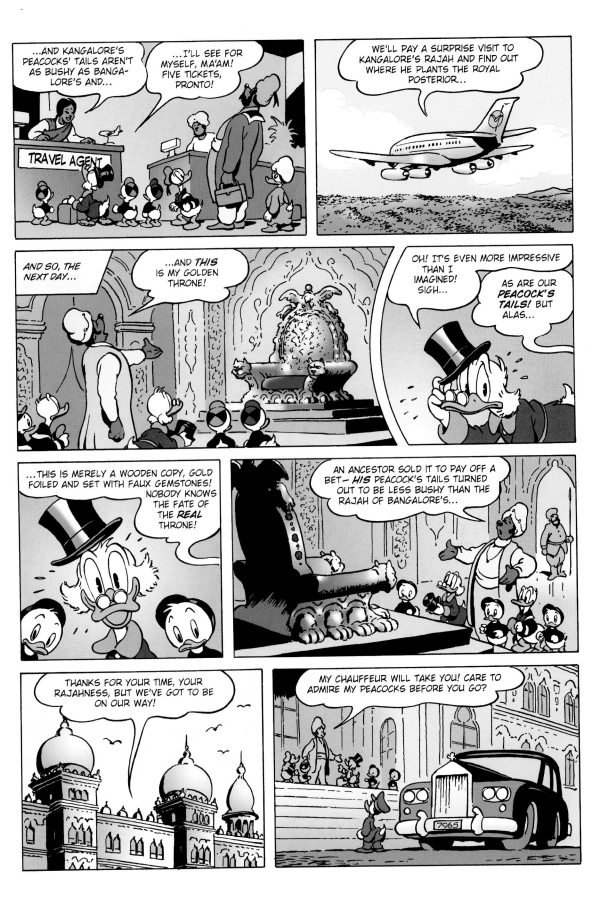

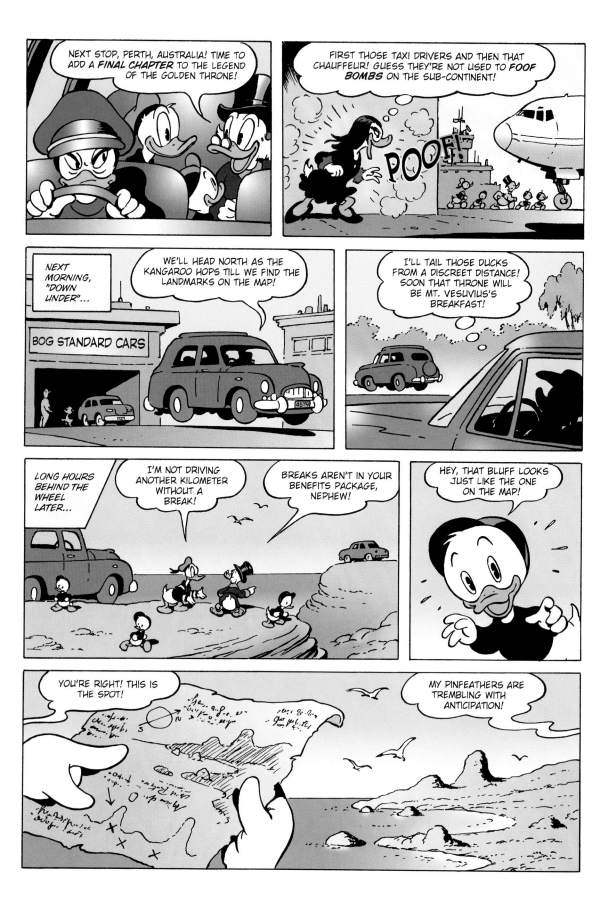

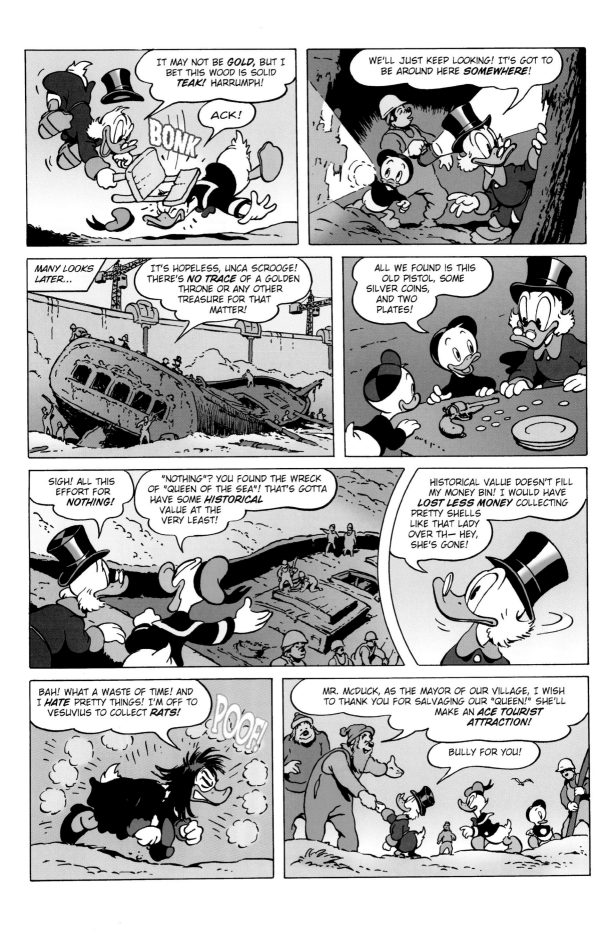

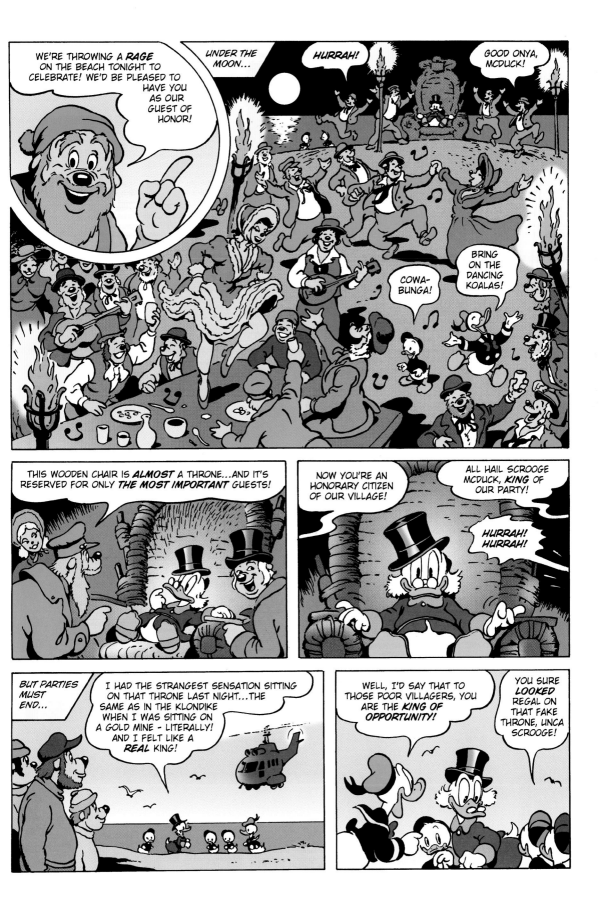

MORE Disney excitement TO COME!

These books are just the first in a series of prestige and regular-format comics that will feature exciting stories and adventures of the Standard Disney Characters that you know and love, including Donald Duck, Uncle Scrooge, Mickey Mouse, Huey, Dewey, and Louie, Gyro Gearloose, and many more.

Now on sale and on a monthly schedule. Walt Disney's Comics and Stories and Walt Disney's Uncle Scrooge, each in 64-page Prestige format for $6.95.

Available July 22, 2003. The first book in Gemstone's new series – Walt Disney's Donald Duck Adventures, a travel-sized pocket book featuring 128 pages of long adventure stories in 5" X 7½" squarebound format for $7.95. These books will be published on a regular basis.

Appearing monthly starting September 9, 2003. Walt Disney's Donald Duck and Walt Disney's Mickey Mouse and Friends (not pictured), each in 32-page newsstand comic format for $2.95

Look for them at your local comic shop! Can't find a comic shop? Try the Toll Free Comic Shop Locator Service at (888) COMIC BOOK for the shop nearest you! If you can't find Gemstone's Disney comics in your neighborhood you may subscribe at no extra charge, and we'll pay the postage! Use the coupon below, or a copy:

©2003 Disney Enterprises, Inc.

BOY, I LOVE SUNDAYS! THE KIDS SLEEP IN AND I GET TO EAT WHAT I WANT FOR BREAKFAST!

EGGS, BACON, SAUSAGE. PANCAKES, FISH BITES, FRIED TOMATOES...! I CALL IT THE DONALD DUCK ALL-WEEK BREAKFAST!

D 2000-121

HOLD ON! SOMETHING'S MISSING! RASP-BERRY JAM? MAPLE SYRUP? LEMON CURD? NO, THAT'S ALL HERE!

KETCHUP! THAT'S IT! A "DONALD DUCK ALL WEEK BREAKFAST" WOULDN'T BE THE SAME WITHOUT A HEARTY DOLLOP OF KETCHUP!

RATS! IT'S STUCK! I CAN'T UNSCREW IT!

THIS CALLS FOR ONE OF DONALD DUCK'S HANDY HOUSEHOLD HINTS! PLACE BOTTLE IN DOOR JAMB, NUDGE DOOR SO IT GRIPS THE CAP AND...

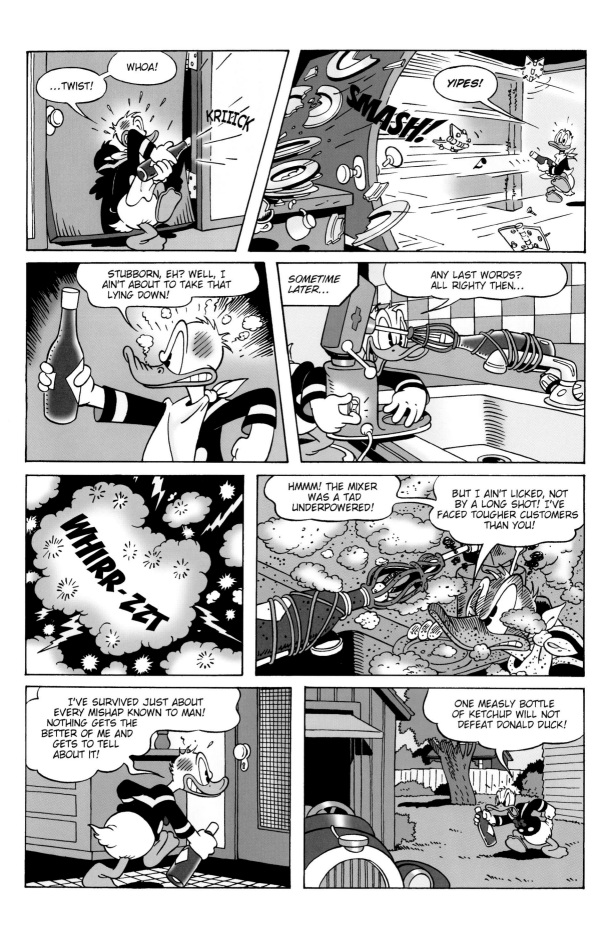

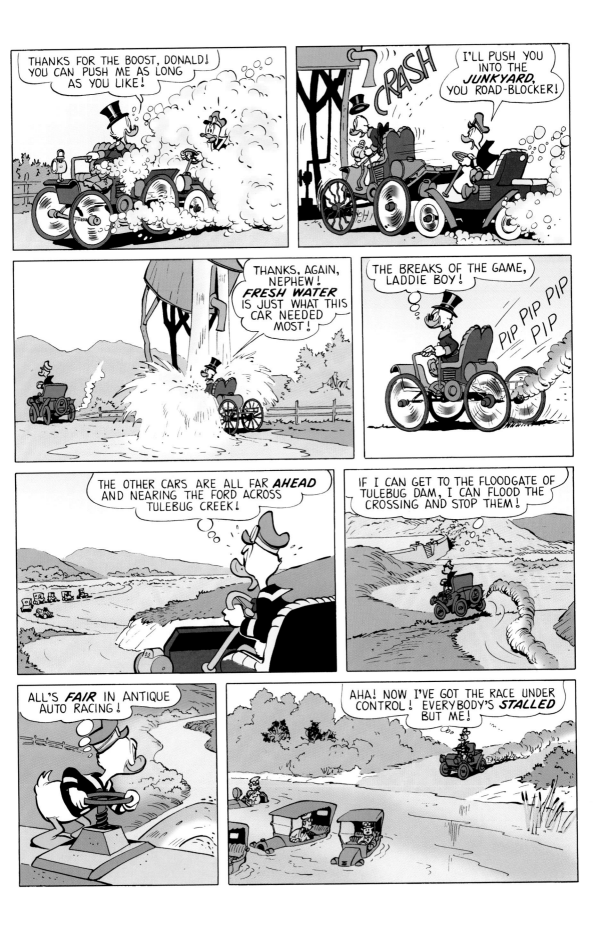

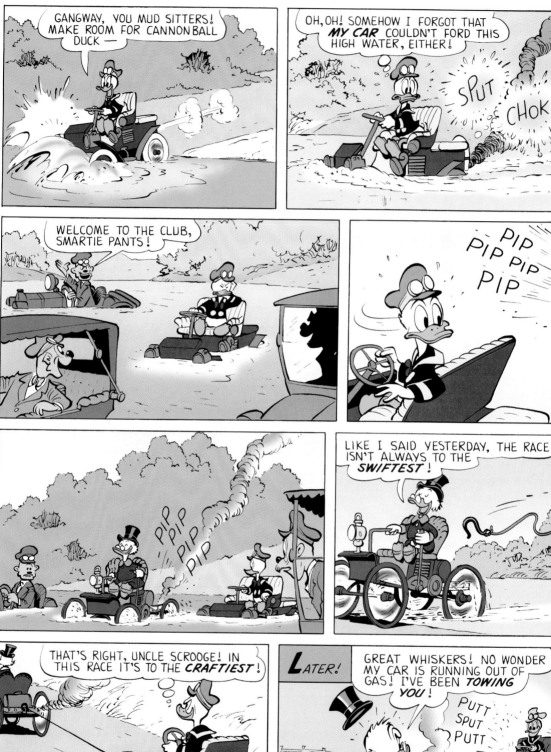

The Screwball Derby

"Chugwagon Derby" is a reworking of a story that Barks originally wrote in 1943. In "The Hard Loser" (**Donald Duck** FC 29), Donald and the nephews compete in a no-holds-barred steeplechase, only to discover at the finish line that the race is not to the swiftest. Collector Malcolm Willits suggested that Barks revive this story using antique cars as the central gimmick.

"I have just finished drawing the new antique-car-race version of the Screwball Derby for the **Uncle Scrooge** comic due on the stands next May," Barks wrote to Willits on

November 17, 1960. "Made it a ten-pager with enough new twists in the gags to keep it from being a copy of the older story. The ending, however, was impossible to top. The fact that the **last** contestant wins is what makes the preceding gags extraordinary. That particular type of race was described to me years ago by a Disney artist from Wisconsin, whose family owned a horse so slow and rheumatic that he always won the plughorse race at the county fairs. The fairs featured the last-horse-wins race as a comic stunt every year."

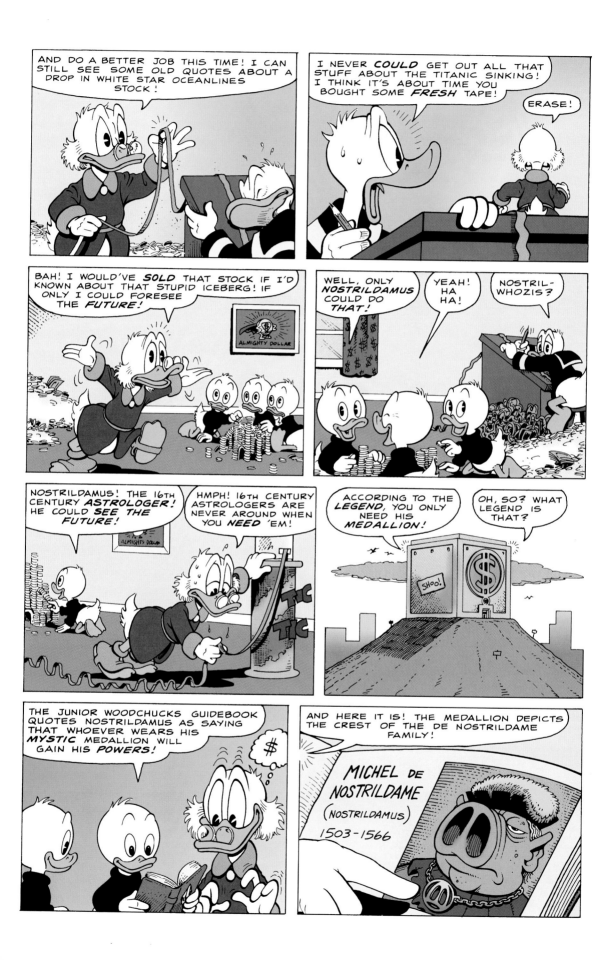

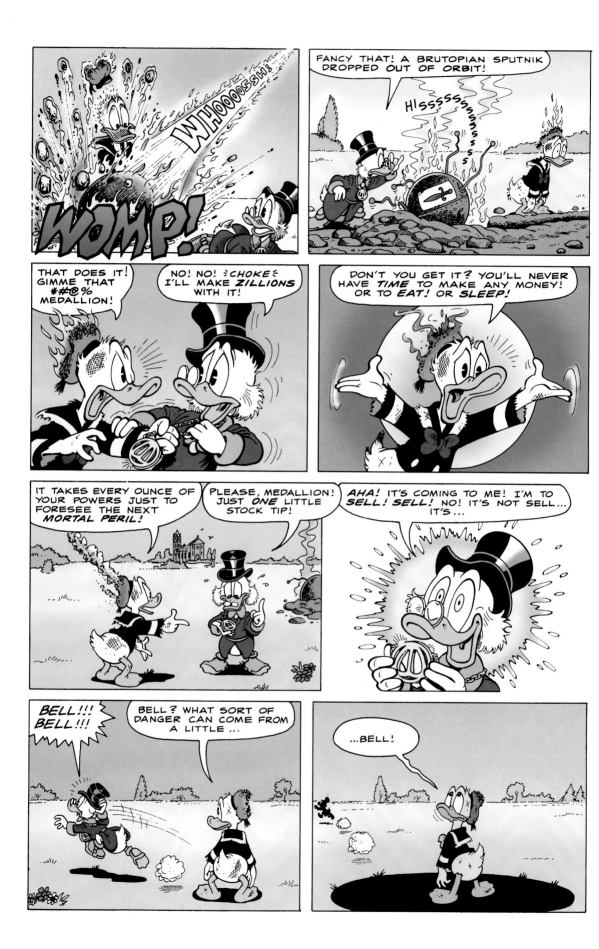

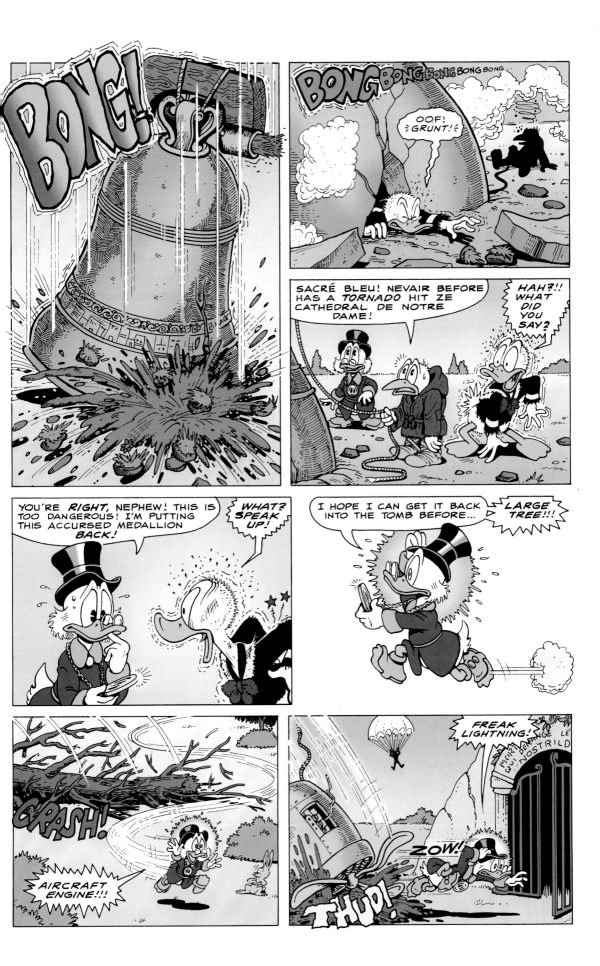

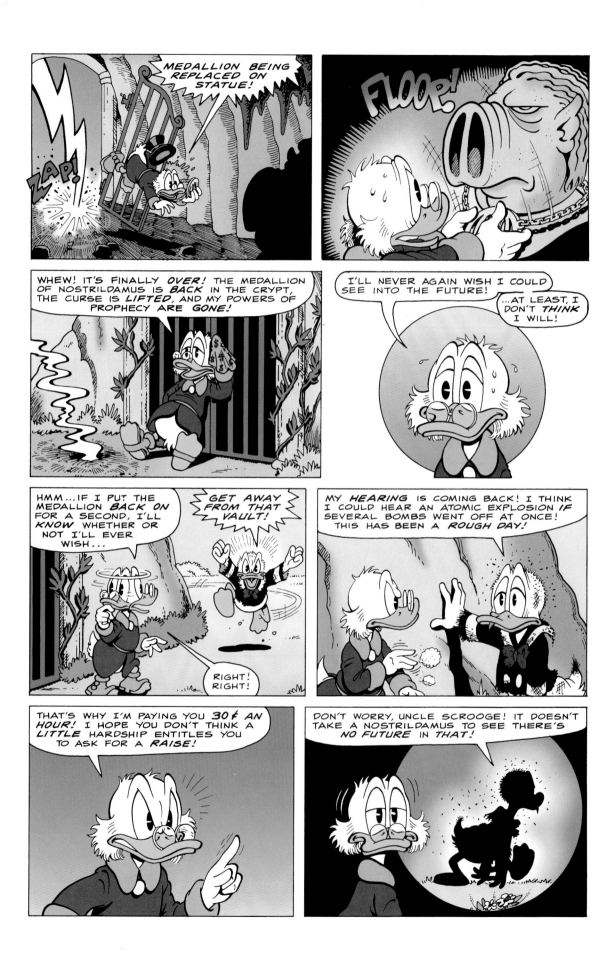

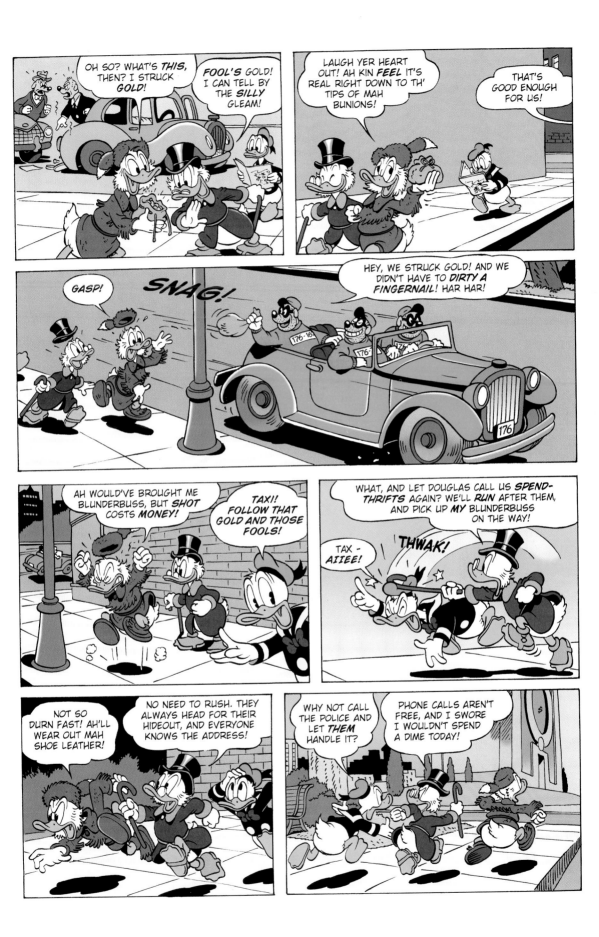

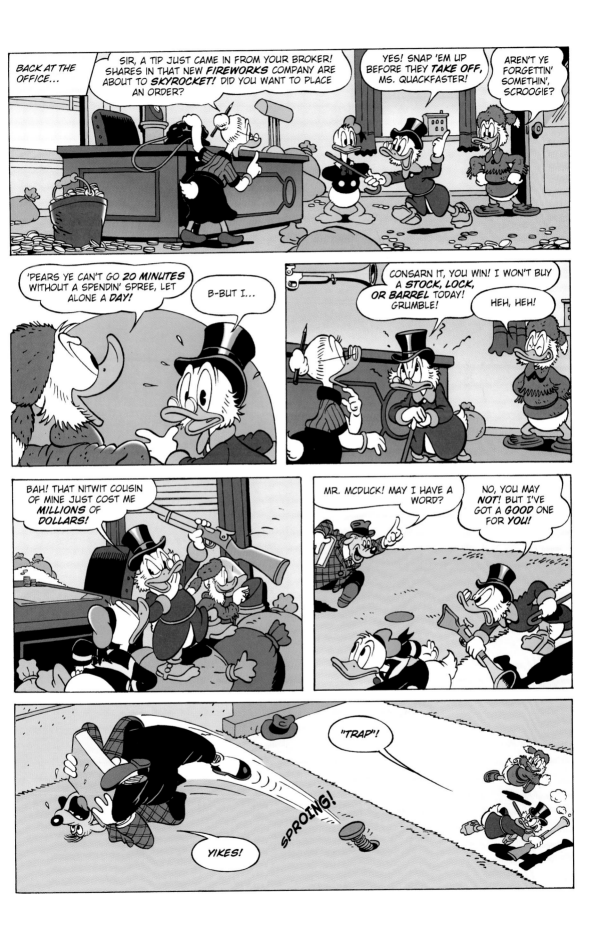

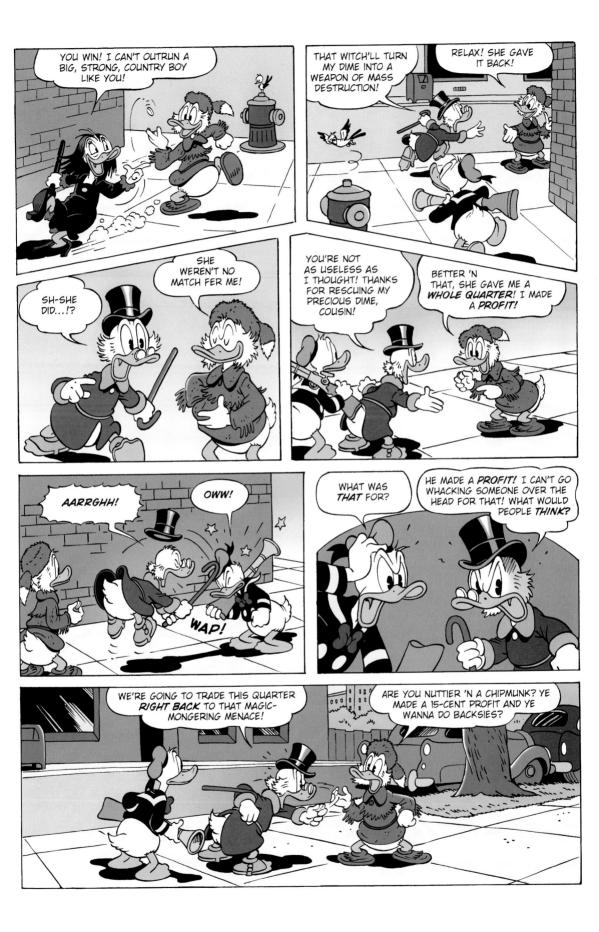

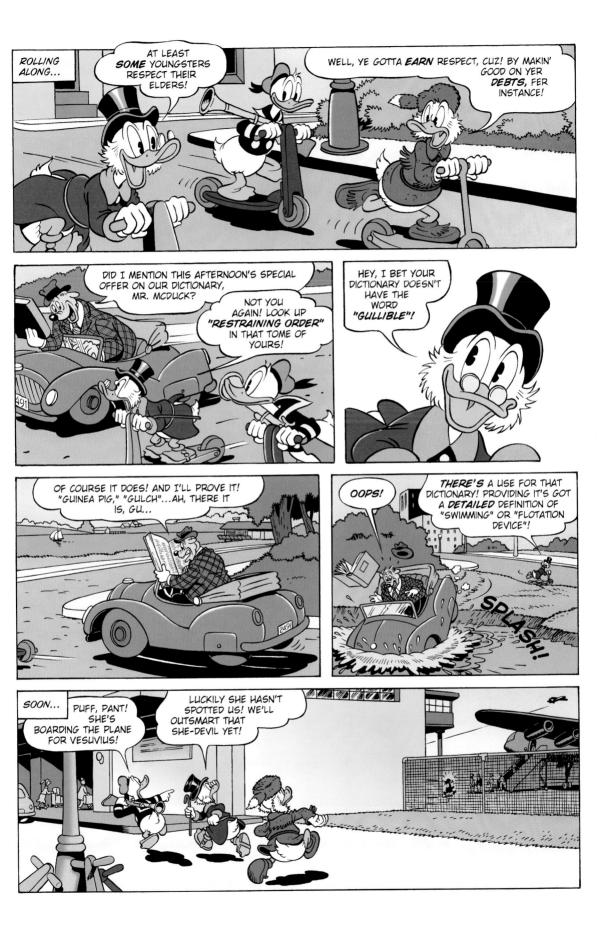